Wedding Planner

Published by Floraison Journals and Planners

This is Us

YOU	ME
Name:	**Name:**
Date of Birth:	**Date of Birth:**
Occupation:	**Occupation:**
Photo	**Photo**

How We Met and the Proposal

Photos

Monthly Planner

January

Sunday	Monday	Tuesday	Wednesday
	○	○	○
○	○	○	○
○	○	○	○
○	○	○	○
○	○	○	○

January

Thursday	Friday	Saturday	Notes
◯	◯	◯	
◯	◯	◯	
◯	◯	◯	
◯	◯	◯	
◯	◯	◯	

February

Sunday	Monday	Tuesday	Wednesday
	○	○	○
○	○	○	○
○	○	○	○
○	○	○	○
○	○	○	○

February

Thursday	Friday	Saturday	Notes
○	○	○	
○	○	○	
○	○	○	
○	○	○	
○	○	○	

March

Sunday	Monday	Tuesday	Wednesday

March

Thursday	Friday	Saturday	Notes
◯	◯	◯	
◯	◯	◯	
◯	◯	◯	
◯	◯	◯	
◯	◯	◯	

April

Sunday	Monday	Tuesday	Wednesday
○	○	○	○
○	○	○	○
○	○	○	○
○	○	○	○
○	○	○	○

April

Thursday	Friday	Saturday	Notes
◯	◯	◯	
◯	◯	◯	
◯	◯	◯	
◯	◯	◯	
◯	◯	◯	

May

Sunday	Monday	Tuesday	Wednesday
○	○	○	○
○	○	○	○
○	○	○	○
○	○	○	○
○	○	○	○

May

Thursday	Friday	Saturday	Notes
○	○	○	
○	○	○	
○	○	○	
○	○	○	
○	○	○	

June

Sunday	Monday	Tuesday	Wednesday
○	○	○	○
○	○	○	○
○	○	○	○
○	○	○	○
○	○	○	○

June

Thursday	Friday	Saturday	Notes
◯	◯	◯	
◯	◯	◯	
◯	◯	◯	
◯	◯	◯	
◯	◯	◯	

July

Sunday	Monday	Tuesday	Wednesday
○	○	○	○
○	○	○	○
○	○	○	○
○	○	○	○
○	○	○	○

July

Thursday	Friday	Saturday	Notes
○	○	○	
○	○	○	
○	○	○	
○	○	○	
○	○	○	

August

Sunday	Monday	Tuesday	Wednesday
○	○	○	○
○	○	○	○
○	○	○	○
○	○	○	○
○	○	○	○

August

Thursday	Friday	Saturday	Notes
○	○	○	
○	○	○	
○	○	○	
○	○	○	
○	○	○	

September

Sunday	Monday	Tuesday	Wednesday

September

Thursday	Friday	Saturday	Notes
○	○	○	
○	○	○	
○	○	○	
○	○	○	
○	○	○	

October

Sunday	Monday	Tuesday	Wednesday
	○	○	○	○
○	○	○	○
○	○	○	○
○	○	○	○
○	○	○	○

October

Thursday	Friday	Saturday	Notes
○	○	○	
○	○	○	
○	○	○	
○	○	○	
○	○	○	

November

Sunday	Monday	Tuesday	Wednesday
○	○	○	○
○	○	○	○
○	○	○	○
○	○	○	○
○	○	○	○

November

Thursday	Friday	Saturday	Notes
○	○	○	
○	○	○	
○	○	○	
○	○	○	
○	○	○	

December

Sunday	Monday	Tuesday	Wednesday
	◯	◯	◯
◯	◯	◯	◯
◯	◯	◯	◯
◯	◯	◯	◯
◯	◯	◯	◯

December

Thursday	Friday	Saturday	Notes
○	○	○	
○	○	○	
○	○	○	
○	○	○	
○	○	○	

1 Week Before

	THINGS TO DO:	NOTES:
MONDAY		
TUESDAY		
WEDNESDAY		
THURSDAY		

REMINDERS & NOTES:

1 Week Before

THINGS TO DO:

NOTES:

FRIDAY

SATURDAY

SUNDAY

LEFT TO DO:

REMINDERS:

NOTES:

Notes

Wedding Plans

12 Months Before

- SET THE DATE
- SET YOUR BUDGET
- CHOOSE YOUR THEME
- ORGANIZE ENGAGEMENT PARTY
- RESEARCH VENUES
- BOOK A WEDDING PLANNER
- RESEARCH PHOTOGRAPHERS
- RESEARCH VIDEOGRAPHERS
- RESEARCH DJ'S/ENTERTAINMENT

- CONSIDER FLORISTS
- RESEARCH CATERERS
- DECIDE ON OFFICIANT
- CREATE INITIAL GUEST LIST
- CHOOSE WEDDING PARTY
- SHOP FOR WEDDING DRESS
- REGISTER WITH GIFT REGISTRY
- DISCUSS HONEYMOON IDEAS
- RESEARCH WEDDING RINGS

THINGS TO REMEMBER:

9 Months Before

- [ ] FINALIZE GUEST LIST
- [ ] ORDER INVITATIONS
- [ ] PLAN YOUR RECEPTION
- [ ] BOOK PHOTOGRAPHER
- [ ] BOOK VIDEOGRAPHER
- [ ] BOOK FLORIST
- [ ] BOOK DJ/ENTERTAINMENT
- [ ] BOOK CATERER
- [ ] CHOOSE WEDDING CAKE

- [ ] CHOOSE WEDDING GOWN
- [ ] ORDER BRIDESMAIDS DRESSES
- [ ] RESERVE TUXEDOS
- [ ] ARRANGE TRANSPORTATION
- [ ] BOOK WEDDING VENUE
- [ ] BOOK RECEPTION VENUE
- [ ] PLAN HONEYMOON
- [ ] BOOK OFFICIANT
- [ ] BOOK ROOMS FOR GUESTS

THINGS TO REMEMBER:

6 Months Before

- ORDER THANK YOU NOTES
- REVIEW RECEPTION DETAILS
- MAKE APPT FOR DRESS FITTING
- CONFIRM BRIDEMAIDS DRESSES
- GET MARRIAGE LICENSE

- BOOK HAIR/MAKE UP STYLIST
- CONFIRM MUSIC SELECTIONS
- PLAN BRIDAL SHOWER
- PLAN REHEARSAL
- SHOP FOR WEDDING RINGS

THINGS TO REMEMBER:

3 Months Before

- MAIL OUT INVITATIONS
- MEET WITH OFFICIANT
- BUY GIFTS FOR WEDDING PARTY
- BOOK FINAL GOWN FITTING
- BUY WEDDING BANDS
- PLAN YOUR HAIR STYLE
- PURCHASE SHOES/HEELS
- CONFIRM PASSPORTS ARE VALID

- FINALIZE RECEPTION MENU
- PLAN REHEARSAL DINNER
- CONFIRM ALL BOOKINGS
- APPLY FOR MARRIAGE LICENSE
- CONFIRM MUSIC SELECTIONS
- DRAFT WEDDING VOWS
- CHOOSE YOUR MC
- ARRANGE AIRPORT TRANSFER

THINGS TO REMEMBER:

1 Month Before

- [ ] CONFIRM FINAL GUEST COUNT
- [ ] CONFIRM RECEPTION DETAILS
- [ ] ATTEND FINAL GOWN FITTING
- [ ] CONFIRM PHOTOGRAPHER
- [ ] WRAP WEDDING PARTY GIFTS
- [ ] CREATE PHOTOGRAPHY SHOT LIST

- [ ] REHEARSE WEDDING VOWS
- [ ] BOOK MANI-PEDI
- [ ] CONFIRM WITH FLORIST
- [ ] CONFIRM VIDEOGRAPHER
- [ ] PICK UP BRIDEMAIDS DRESSES
- [ ] CREATE WEDDING SCHEDULE

THINGS TO REMEMBER:

1 Week Before

- FINALIZE SEATING PLANS
- MAKE PAYMENTS TO VENDORS
- PACK FOR HONEYMOON
- CONFIRM HOTEL RESERVATIONS
- GIVE SCHEDULE TO PARTY

- DELIVER LICENSE TO OFFICIANT
- CONFIRM WITH BAKERY
- PICK UP WEDDING DRESS
- PICK UP TUXEDOS
- GIVE MUSIC LIST TO DJ

THINGS TO REMEMBER:

1 Day Before

- [ ] GET MANICURE/PEDICURE
- [ ] ATTEND REHEARSAL DINNER
- [ ] GET A GOOD NIGHT'S SLEEP!
- [ ] GIVE GIFTS TO WEDDING PARTY
- [ ] FINALIZE PACKING

TO DO LIST:

The Big Day!

- [ ] GET HAIR & MAKE UP DONE
- [ ] HAVE A HEALTHY BREAKFAST
- [ ] ENJOY YOUR BIG DAY!

- [ ] MEET WITH BRIDESMAIDS
- [ ] GIVE RINGS TO BEST MAN

TO DO LIST:

Wedding Day Itinerary

5 am

6 am

7 am

8 am

9 am

10 am

11 am

12 am

1 pm

2 pm

3 pm

4 pm

5 pm

6 pm

7 pm

8 pm

9 pm

10 pm

11pm

12 pm

Wedding Party

MAID/MATRON OF HONOR:

PHONE: DRESS SIZE: SHOE SIZE:

EMAIL:

BRIDESMAID:

PHONE: DRESS SIZE: SHOE SIZE:

EMAIL:

BRIDESMAID #2:

PHONE: DRESS SIZE: SHOE SIZE:

EMAIL:

BRIDESMAID #3:

PHONE: DRESS SIZE: SHOE SIZE:

EMAIL:

BRIDESMAID #4:

PHONE: DRESS SIZE: SHOE SIZE:

EMAIL:

NOTES:

Wedding Party

BEST MAN:

PHONE: WAIST SIZE: SHOE SIZE:

NECK SIZE: SLEEVE SIZE: JACKET SIZE:

EMAIL:

GROOMSMEN #1:

PHONE: WAIST SIZE: SHOE SIZE:

NECK SIZE: SLEEVE SIZE: JACKET SIZE:

EMAIL:

GROOMSMEN #2:

PHONE: WAIST SIZE: SHOE SIZE:

NECK SIZE: SLEEVE SIZE: JACKET SIZE:

EMAIL:

GROOMSMEN #3:

PHONE: WAIST SIZE: SHOE SIZE:

NECK SIZE: SLEEVE SIZE: JACKET SIZE:

EMAIL:

GROOMSMEN #4:

PHONE: WAIST SIZE: SHOE SIZE:

NECK SIZE: SLEEVE SIZE: JACKET SIZE:

EMAIL:

Wedding Planner

ENGAGEMENT PARTY:

DATE: LOCATION: _____

TIME: NUMBER OF GUESTS:

NOTES:

BRIDAL SHOWER:

DATE: _____   LOCATION:

TIME: _____   NUMBER OF GUESTS:

NOTES:

STAG & DOE PARTY:

DATE: LOCATION: _____

TIME: NUMBER OF GUESTS:

NOTES:

Wedding Planner

BACHELORETTE PARTY:

DATE:

LOCATION:

TIME:

NUMBER OF GUESTS:

NOTES:

BACHELOR PARTY:

DATE:

LOCATION:

TIME:

NUMBER OF GUESTS:

NOTES:

CEREMONY REHEARSAL:

DATE:

LOCATION:

TIME:

NUMBER OF GUESTS:

NOTES:

Wedding Planner

REHEARSAL DINNER:

DATE: LOCATION: _____

TIME: NUMBER OF GUESTS:

NOTES:

RECEPTION:

DATE: _____   LOCATION:

TIME: _____   NUMBER OF GUESTS: _____

NOTES:

REMINDERS:

Menu Planner

HORS D'OEUVRES

1st COURSE:

2nd COURSE:

3rd COURSE:

4th COURSE:

DESSERT:

Transportation Planner

TO CEREMONY:　　　PICK UP TIME:　　　PICK UP LOCATION:

BRIDE:

GROOM:

BRIDE'S PARENTS:

GROOM'S PARENTS:

BRIDESMAIDS:

GROOMSMEN:

NOTES:

TO RECEPTION:　　　PICK UP TIME:　　　PICK UP LOCATION:

BRIDE & GROOM:

BRIDE'S PARENTS:

GROOM'S PARENTS:

BRIDESMAIDS:

GROOMSMEN:

Wedding Planner

WEDDING DATE & TIME:

VENUE ADDRESS:

BUDGET:

OFFICIANT:

WEDDING PARTY:

TO DO LIST:

NOTES & REMINDERS:

Vision Boards

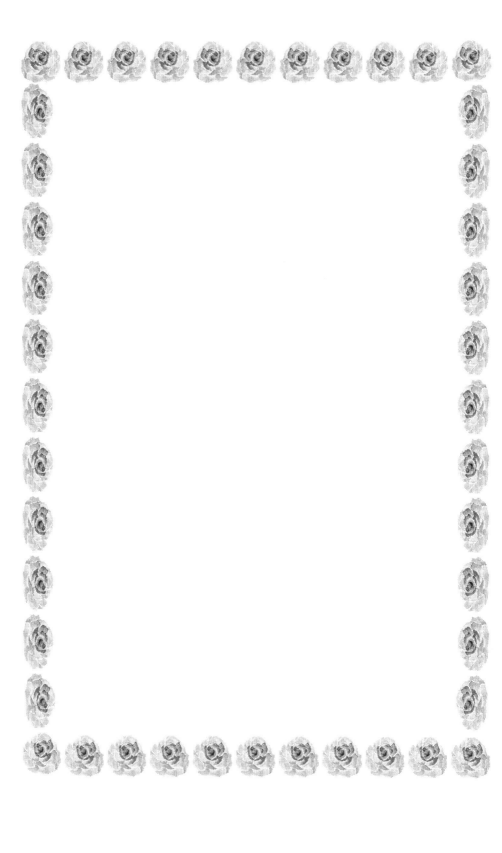

Vendors

Photographer

PHOTOGRAPHER:

PHONE: COMPANY:

EMAIL: ADDRESS:

WEDDING PACKAGE OVERVIEW:

EST PRICE:

INCLUSIONS:	YES ✓	NO ✓	COST:
ENGAGEMENT SHOOT:			
PHOTO ALBUMS:			
FRAMES:			
PROOFS INCLUDED:			
NEGATIVES INCLUDED:			

TOTAL COST:

Videographer

VIDEOGRAPHER:

PHONE: COMPANY:

EMAIL: ADDRESS:

WEDDING PACKAGE OVERVIEW:

EST PRICE:

INCLUSIONS:	YES ✓	NO ✓	COST:
DUPLICATES/COPIES:			
PHOTO MONTAGE:			
MUSIC ADDED:			
EDITING:			

TOTAL COST:

NOTES:

DJ Entertainment

DJ/LIVE BAND/ENTERTAINMENT:

PHONE: COMPANY:

EMAIL: ADDRESS:

START TIME: END TIME:

ENTERTAINMENT SERVICE OVERVIEW:

EST PRICE:

INCLUSIONS:	YES ✓	NO ✓	COST:
SOUND EQUIPMENT:			
LIGHTING:			
SPECIAL EFFECTS:			
GRATUITIES			

TOTAL COST:

NOTES:

Florist

FLORIST:

PHONE: COMPANY: ....

EMAIL: ....   ADDRESS: ....

FLORAL PACKAGE:

EST PRICE:

INCLUSIONS:	YES ✓	NO ✓	COST:
BRIDAL BOUQUET:			
THROW AWAY BOUQUET:			
CORSAGES:			
CEREMONY FLOWERS			
CENTERPIECES			
CAKE TOPPER			
BOUTONNIERE			

TOTAL COST:

Wedding Cake/ Baker

PHONE: _____   COMPANY: _____

EMAIL: _____   ADDRESS: _____

WEDDING CAKE PACKAGE:

COST: _____ FREE TASTING: _____ DELIVERY FEE: _____

FLAVOR:

FILLING:

SIZE:

SHAPE:

COLOR:

EXTRAS:

TOTAL COST:

NOTES:

Caterer Details

CONTACT INFORMATION:

PHONE: _____   CONTACT NAME:

EMAIL: ADDRESS:

MENU CHOICE #1:

MENU CHOICE #2:

	YES ✓	NO ✓	COST:
BAR INCLUDED:			
CORKAGE FEE:			
HORS D'OEUVRES:			
TAXES INCLUDED:			
GRATUITIES INCLUDED:			

Names & Addresses

CEREMONY:

PHONE: _____   CONTACT NAME:

EMAIL: ADDRESS:

RECEPTION:

PHONE: _____   CONTACT NAME:

EMAIL: ADDRESS:

OFFICIANT:

PHONE: _____   CONTACT NAME:

EMAIL: ADDRESS:

WEDDING PLANNER:

PHONE: CONTACT NAME: _____

EMAIL: _____   ADDRESS: _____

CATERER:

PHONE: _____   CONTACT NAME: _____

EMAIL: ADDRESS: _____

FLORIST:

PHONE: CONTACT NAME: _____

EMAIL: _____   ADDRESS:

Names & Addresses

BAKERY:

PHONE: _____   CONTACT NAME:

EMAIL: ADDRESS: _____

BRIDAL SHOP:

PHONE: _____   CONTACT NAME:

EMAIL: ADDRESS:

PHOTOGRAPHER:

PHONE: _____   CONTACT NAME:

EMAIL: ADDRESS:

VIDEOGRAPHER:

PHONE: CONTACT NAME: _____

EMAIL: _____   ADDRESS:

DJ/ENTERTAINMENT:

PHONE: CONTACT NAME: _____

EMAIL: _____   ADDRESS: _____

HAIR/NAIL SALON:

PHONE: CONTACT NAME:

EMAIL: _____   ADDRESS: _____

Names & Addresses

MAKE UP ARTIST:

PHONE: _____   CONTACT NAME:

EMAIL: _____   ADDRESS:

RENTALS:

PHONE: _____   CONTACT NAME: _____

EMAIL: _____   ADDRESS:

HONEYMOON RESORT/HOTEL:

PHONE: _____   CONTACT NAME: _____

EMAIL: _____   ADDRESS: _____

TRANSPORTATION SERVICE:

PHONE: _____   CONTACT NAME:

EMAIL: _____   ADDRESS: _____

NOTES:

Lists

Wedding Guest List

NAME:	ADDRESS:	# IN PARTY:	RSVP: ✓

Wedding Guest List

NAME:	ADDRESS:	# IN PARTY:	RSVP: ✓

Wedding Guest List

NAME:	ADDRESS:	# IN PARTY:	RSVP: ✓

Wedding Guest List

NAME:	ADDRESS:	# IN PARTY:	RSVP: ✓

Wedding Guest List

NAME:	ADDRESS:	# IN PARTY:	RSVP: ✓

Wedding Guest List

NAME:	ADDRESS:	# IN PARTY:	RSVP: ✓

Wedding Guest List

NAME:	ADDRESS:	# IN PARTY:	RSVP: ✓

Wedding Guest List

NAME:	ADDRESS:	# IN PARTY:	RSVP: ✓

Seating Chart Planner

Table #

Table #	
1:	
2:	
3:	
4:	
5:	
6:	
7:	
8:	

Table #

Table #	
1:	
2:	
3:	
4:	
5:	
6:	
7:	
8:	

SEATING PLANNER NOTES:

Seating Chart Planner

Table #

Table #	
1:	
2:	
3:	
4:	
5:	
6:	
7:	
8:	

Table #

Table #	
1:	
2:	
3:	
4:	
5:	
6:	
7:	
8:	

SEATING PLANNER NOTES:

Seating Chart Planner

Table #

Table #	
1:	
2:	
3:	
4:	
5:	
6:	
7:	
8:	

Table #

Table #	
1:	
2:	
3:	
4:	
5:	
6:	
7:	
8:	

SEATING PLANNER NOTES:

Seating Chart Planner

Table #	
1:	
2:	
3:	
4:	
5:	
6:	
7:	
8:	

Table #

Table #	
1:	
2:	
3:	
4:	
5:	
6:	
7:	
8:	

Table #

SEATING PLANNER NOTES:

Seating Chart Planner

Table #	
1:	
2:	
3:	
4:	
5:	
6:	
7:	
8:	

Table #	
1:	
2:	
3:	
4:	
5:	
6:	
7:	
8:	

SEATING PLANNER NOTES:

Seating Chart Planner

Table #

Table #	
1:	
2:	
3:	
4:	
5:	
6:	
7:	
8:	

Table #

Table #	
1:	
2:	
3:	
4:	
5:	
6:	
7:	
8:	

SEATING PLANNER NOTES:

Seating Chart Planner

Table #

Table #	
1:	
2:	
3:	
4:	
5:	
6:	
7:	
8:	

Table #

Table #	
1:	
2:	
3:	
4:	
5:	
6:	
7:	
8:	

SEATING PLANNER NOTES:

Seating Chart Planner

Table #

Table #	
1:	
2:	
3:	
4:	
5:	
6:	
7:	
8:	

Table #

Table #	
1:	
2:	
3:	
4:	
5:	
6:	
7:	
8:	

SEATING PLANNER NOTES:

Seating Chart Planner

Table #

Table #	
1:	
2:	
3:	
4:	
5:	
6:	
7:	
8:	

Table #

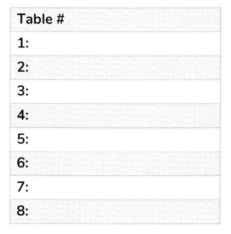

Table #	
1:	
2:	
3:	
4:	
5:	
6:	
7:	
8:	

SEATING PLANNER NOTES:

Seating Chart Planner

Table #

Table #	
1:	
2:	
3:	
4:	
5:	
6:	
7:	
8:	

Table #

Table #	
1:	
2:	
3:	
4:	
5:	
6:	
7:	
8:	

SEATING PLANNER NOTES:

Gift Log

NAME	GIFT	THANK YOU CARD SENT

Gift Log

NAME	GIFT	THANK YOU CARD SENT

Gift Log

NAME	GIFT	THANK YOU CARD SENT

Gift Log

NAME	GIFT	THANK YOU CARD SENT

Gift Log

NAME	GIFT	THANK YOU CARD SENT

Gift Log

NAME	GIFT	THANK YOU CARD SENT

Gift Log

NAME	GIFT	THANK YOU CARD SENT

Gift Log

NAME	GIFT	THANK YOU CARD SENT

Song / Music List

Ceremony

Title	Artist	Duration

Reception - Entrance

Title	Artist	Duration

First Dance

Title	Artist	Duration

Parent Dances

Title	Artist	Duration

Song/Music List

Father-Daughter Dance

Title	Artist	Duration

Mother-Son Dance

Title	Artist	Duration

Cake Cutting

Title	Artist	Duration

Bouquet Toss

Title	Artist	Duration

Garter Toss

Title	Artist	Duration

Song/Music List

Hit the Dance Floor!

Title	Artist	Duration

Last Dance

Title	Artist	Duration

Song/Music List

Our Favorites

Title	Artist	Duration

Don't Play List

Title	Artist	Duration

Wedding Day Emergency Kit

Description	Packed
Travel sewing kit	
Thread	
Safety pins	
Small scissors	
Double sided tape (keeps clothes in place)	
Lint roller	
Stick-on instant hemming tape	
Clear nail polish	
White chalk (Masks wedding dress stains)	
Pain reliever	
Antacids	
Diarrhea medication	
Antiseptic lotion	
Bandages	
Band-aids	
Breath mints	
Dental floss	
Deodorant	
Perfume	

Wedding Day Emergency Kit

Description	Packed
Oil absorbing sheets	
Cotton swabs	
Tissues	
Tweezers	
Lip balm	
Hand Lotion	
Emery board	
Bobby pins	
Comb	
Hairspray	
Nail Polish (Bride's Color)	
Nail Glue	
Small mirror	
Foundation	
Powder	
Mascara	
Eyeliner	
Eye shadow	
Lipstick	
Lip gloss	

Wedding Party Gifts

GIFT FOR:	GIFT:	COST: ✓
Maid of Honor		
Best Man		
Bridesmaids		
Groomsmen		

Wedding Party Gifts

GIFT FOR:	GIFT:	COST: ✓
Ring Bearer		
Flower Girl		
Family		

Wedding Budget

	TOTAL COST:	DEPOSIT:	REMAINDER:
WEDDING VENUE			
RECEPTION VENUE			
FLORIST			
OFFICIANT			
CATERER			
WEDDING CAKE			
BRIDAL ATTIRE			
GROOM ATTIRE			
BRIDAL JEWELRY			
BRIDESMAID ATTIRE			
GROOMSMEN ATTIRE			
HAIR & MAKE UP			
PHOTOGRAPHER			
VIDEOGRAPHER			
DJ SERVICE/ENTERTAINMENT			
INVITATIONS			
TRANSPORTATION			
WEDDING PARTY GIFTS			
RENTALS			
HONEYMOON			

Wedding Budget

	TOTAL COST:	DEPOSIT:	REMAINDER:

Wedding Budget

	TOTAL COST:	DEPOSIT:	REMAINDER:

Honeymoon

Honeymoon Details

Departure

Destination

Airline _____   Flight Number _____

Connection _____   Arrive _____

Departure

Destination

Airline _____   Flight Number _____

Connection _____   Arrive _____

Departure

Destination

Airline _____   Flight Number _____

Connection _____   Arrive _____

Departure

Destination

Airline _____   Flight Number _____

Connection _____   Arrive _____

Honeymoon Details

RENTAL CAR

Company

Address

Make & Model

Pick-up   Drop-off

HOTELS

Name

Address

Check-in   Check-out

Name

Address

Check-in   Check-out

Name

Address

Check-in   Check-out

Honeymoon Budget

	TOTAL COST:	DEPOSIT:	REMAINDER:

Honeymoon Budget

	TOTAL COST:	DEPOSIT:	REMAINDER:

Honeymoon Travel Basics

DESCRIPTION:	PACKED:
CARRY-ON (if applicable)	
Passports, Visas	
Picture I.D. (e.g. Driver's License)	
Travel Insurance Information	
Health Insurance Card	
Reservation Confirmations (hotels, rental cars etc)	
Airline Tickets/E-Tickets	
Boarding Passes	
Credit Cards (only the ones you intend to use)	
ATM Cards	
Cash (small amount of local currency for taxis etc)	
Travel Itinerary	
List of Contacts (doctors, credit card companies etc)	
Photocopies of Passports, Visas, etc (stored separately)	
Scan all important documents (Passports etc) store in the cloud	
Vaccinations	
Medication (in original containers)	
Birth Control	
Motion Sickness Medication	
Jewelry	

Honeymoon Travel Basics

DESCRIPTION:	PACKED:
CARRY-ON (con't)	
Laptop (fully charged)	
Ipad/Tablet (fully charged)	
Cell Phone (fully charged)	
Portable Chargers	
Travel Plug Adapter	
Electrical Converter Adapter (if required)	
Headphones	
Eyeglasses	
Sunglasses	
Camera	
Books, magazines	

Leave with someone you trust:

•Photocopies of any important documents such as Passports, Visas, Drivers' Licenses, Travel Insurance, Health Insurance Cards, Reservation Confirmation Numbers etc

•Name, addresses and phone numbers of accommodation with the check-in and check-out dates

•A List of emergency contacts and any other important contact information

Honeymoon Packing List

CLOTHES:	PACKED:

Honeymoon Packing List

CLOTHES:	PACKED:

Honeymoon Packing List

ACCESSORIES:	PACKED:

Honeymoon Packing List

TOILETRIES:	PACKED:

Honeymoon Packing List

TOILETRIES:	PACKED:

Honeymoon Notes

Notes

Notes

Notes

Notes

Notes

Our Vows

Our Vows

Made in the USA
Monee, IL
15 January 2020